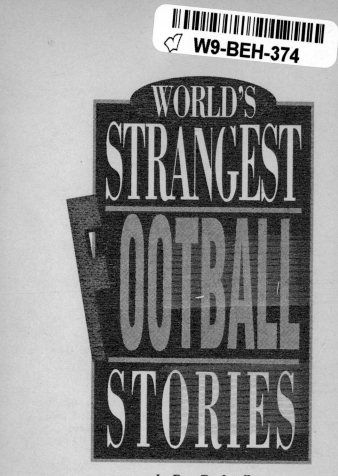

WORLD'S STRANGEST FOOTBALL STORIES

by Bart Rockwell

Watermill Press

Metric Equivalents

1 inch	= 2.540 centimeters
1 foot	= 0.305 meters
1 yard	= 0.914 meters
1 mile	= 1.609 kilometers
1 pound	= 0.45 kilograms

To Jim and Matt

Cover illustration by Paulette Bogan

LIBRARY OF CONGRESS CATALOGING-IN-PUBLICATION DATA

Rockwell, Bart, (date)
   World's strangest football stories / by Bart Rockwell.
      p.   cm.
   Summary: Relates unusual stories and facts from football history.
   ISBN 0-8167-2934-4 (lib. bdg.)   ISBN 0-8167-2851-8 (pbk.)
   1. Football—United States—Anecdotes—Juvenile literature.
   [1. Football—Miscellanea.   2. Football—History.]   I. Title.
GV950.7.R63   1993
796.332'0973—dc20   92-10121

Copyright © 1993 by Watermill Press.
All rights reserved. No part of this book may be used or reproduced in
any manner whatsoever without written permission from the publisher.
Printed in the United States of America.
10 9 8 7 6 5 4 3 2 1

BAND AID

One of the oddest touchdowns in football history occurred in a game between the University of California Golden Bears and Stanford University in November 1982. Stanford was leading 20–19 with four seconds left to play. Stanford then kicked off to California. The ball was fielded by a California player, who threw a lateral pass as he was about to be tackled. At that point, time ran out, but the game was not over because play had not stopped. California players then threw laterals again and again to avoid getting tackled by Stanford defenders. Down the field went California with no time remaining on the clock. Meanwhile the Stanford band, thinking the game was over, marched out onto the field from the Stanford end zone. After five laterals, the ball was in the hands of California's Kevin Moen. Moen raced through the startled Stanford band and into the end zone to score the winning touchdown. California won the game 25–20! It was one of the most bizarre football finishes in the history of the sport.

SET AN EXAMPLE, COACH

On November 10, 1973 two excellent New Jersey high school football teams—Brick Township and Montclair—met in a hotly contested football match-up. Late in the game, a Brick defender picked off a Montclair pass and headed toward the goal line with the intercepted ball. As he raced past the Montclair bench, someone on the sidelines who couldn't control himself ran out onto the field and tackled the Brick player. Strangely enough, the illegal tackler wasn't a player. It was one of the Montclair assistant coaches!

BUSY BOY

Ken Hall of Sugar Land High School in Texas had quite a football career. From 1950 to 1953, Hall rushed for 11,232 yards, including 4,045 yards in 12 games during his senior year! Ken may have been the best high school running back ever. He once gained 520 yards in 11 carries in a single game—an average of over 47 yards per run! Strangely, however, Ken Hall never made headlines as a college player.

FOR SAFETY'S SAKE

Only a handful of NFL defensive players have ever scored two safeties in a season. On October 21, 1973 Los Angeles Rams' defensive end Fred Dryer tackled opposing Green Bay Packer players in the end zone *twice in the same game,* to score two safeties in one contest!

QUEEN FOR A GAME

In November 1990 Amy Cook of Chaminade High School was honored by her fellow students by being voted the school's homecoming queen. Amy wore a white sequined dress and pumps to receive her award, which was presented on the school's football field just before a game. Minutes after she received the homecoming bouquet, Cook rushed into a nearby locker room to put on her football pads, helmet, and uniform. As quick as a flash the homecoming queen rejoined the boys on the sidelines. Amy was the varsity placekicker for the school football team. In fact, a short time after the homecoming-queen ceremonies ended, her team scored, and Amy booted the extra point!

BAD NEWS

New York's Manhattan College, not known for being a football powerhouse, scored one of its biggest football victories ever when it defeated State University of New York—Maritime College by the score of 31–0 in 1980. Manhattan players and fans rejoiced over the big win and couldn't wait to read about the big upset victory the next day in the newspapers.

Unfortunately, their joy was short-lived. The *New York Times* got the school's name wrong, reporting the game as a 31–0 victory for *Manhattanville* College. Even worse, another area newspaper reported the score as Maritime 31, Manhattan 0! It just goes to prove you can't believe everything you read in the newspapers.

WRONG TURN

Turk Edwards was a tough tackle for the Washington Redskins in the late 1930's and early 1940's. A member of the Football Hall of Fame, Turk had the misfortune to suffer an injury in 1940 that ended his career. What is so strange about Edwards' injury is that it occurred during the coin toss of a game between the Redskins and the New York Giants. Edwards was captain of the Washington squad. Before the game, he met out on the field with the referee and Mel Heim, the captain of the Giants. After the coin toss, Turk turned to go back to the Redskins' sideline. As he turned, his football cleats stuck in the turf and he severely twisted his knee. He was carried off the field in great pain. The knee never got better, and Turk Edwards' 12-year NFL career was brought to an abrupt end.

WACKY RULE

Did you know that it used to be illegal to pass the pigskin in the game of football? It's true. Throwing a forward pass was illegal until 1905.

TAKEN FOR A RIDE

In 1973, the Cheyney (Pennsylvania) State College football team was really taken for a ride when it traveled to California (Pennsylvania) State College for an away game. The trouble began when the team's chartered bus showed up. The bus could hold only 46 people, too small for the 52 players the Cheyney State coach wanted to bring to the game. Six players had to be left behind. On the way to the game, the bus caught fire and its engine broke down. A new bus had to be called to pick up the team, and after a two-hour wait, that bus arrived. Then, after the journey was resumed, a door on the second bus fell off! The Cheyney State coach was quite upset when his team finally arrived. But he was even more upset after the game. Cheyney State lost to California State, 3–0!

DON'T BADGER ME!

The Wisconsin Badgers started a new football trend in October 1981. For the first time since 1959, the Badgers defeated the Ohio State Buckeyes, ending a 21-game losing streak to Ohio State.

ZERO OUTPUT

The Big Bay De Noc High School football team of Cook, Michigan had a terrible season in 1979. In fact, their season was so bad that the team established a record that might be tough to break. That record was for having the most consecutive points scored against a team without that team scoring any points itself. Over a 13-game span, Big Bay De Noc gave up 728 points to opponents, while scoring none itself!

PSYCHE OUT

Mind over matter may work in some instances, but apparently not when it comes to football. In 1979 a group of 12 gifted psychics got together to predict the outcome of that year's Super Bowl, which pitted the Dallas Cowboys against the Pittsburgh Steelers. Nine of the twelve psychics insisted that Dallas was a cinch to beat Pittsburgh in football's ultimate match-up. Unfortunately, the psychics may have been "out of their minds" when they made their predictions. Pittsburgh ended up defeating Dallas, 35–31.

RECORD TROPHY

In 1979, Philadelphia Eagles wide receiver Harold Carmichael set a record (since broken) by catching passes in 106 consecutive NFL games. For his efforts Carmichael was awarded a trophy— and it was a big one. To commemorate the feat, Carmichael was given a trophy that stood 23 feet, 9 inches tall. The trophy was so large that it even received a mention in the *Guinness Book of World Records*. Now that's a big-time football award!

BALL TRICK

Johnny Rodgers made the big play for the
Montreal Alouettes in a Canadian Football
League playoff game against the Toronto Argonauts
on November 12, 1973. Rodgers caught a touchdown
pass late in the contest that iced the win for the
Alouettes. Excited by the prospect of a playoff
victory, Rodgers threw the ball into the screaming
crowd.

After the touchdown the teams lined up for the
extra point. But there was a problem. The extra point
couldn't be attempted. There was no football!
Rodgers had tossed the last game ball into the stands.
There wasn't another football to be found anywhere.
Strangely enough, the game had to be ended without
the pat!

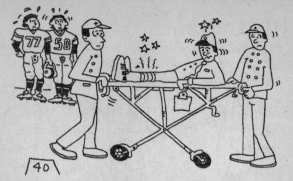

COACH CRASH

When Dan Devine left the University of Missouri to take charge of the Green Bay Packers, he knew coaching in the NFL would be tough. But he also knew that moving from the college ranks to the pros was a big break for his career.

In his coaching debut against the New York Giants, Devine learned just how big a break the change really was. While standing on the sidelines during the game, the new coach got in the way of a Giants player who was running out of bounds, and the collision broke Devine's leg. To make things even worse, the Giants broke into the win column that day with a 42–40 victory over the Packers.

NO LOCK

When the Rutgers University football team traveled to West Virginia for a contest against the West Virginia Mountaineers in November 1991, the Scarlet Knights had a tough time getting onto the field at game time. In fact, the Rutgers squad was almost late for the kickoff, because they'd somehow gotten locked in their locker room!

DRIVING DOWN THE FIELD

F ootball fans in the New York area weren't too happy with the poor play of the New York Giants in 1980. When the Giants took on the Cardinals that season, there was a big traffic jam leaving Giants Stadium. The problem is, the traffic jam occurred at halftime!

NAME GAME

I ndianapolis Colts' football player Brian DeRoo roomed with fellow Colt Randy Burke in 1979. After DeRoo played a season for the Baltimore Colts he decided to get married in 1980. Strangely enough, his fiancee's name was Randee Burke.

TOUGH TUMMY

T he Oregon State Beavers had some real injury problems when they played the University of Minnesota in 1978. The Beavers had lost their first-, second-, and third-team defensive tackles during the game to injuries. That's enough to give a coach stomach trouble. And stomach trouble is what Oregon State defensive tackle #4 had when he entered the game. After dropping the Minnesota quarterback for a loss, he turned around and threw up on a Minnesota offensive tackle.

LIGHTS OUT

In more and more states across America, high school football games are being played at night. Some players and coaches believe playing at night can help motivate a team. Unfortunately, there wasn't quite enough motivation for the Middlesex, New Jersey high school football team when they played a night game at home on September 6, 1989.

Middlesex was trailing Roselle Park by the score of 13–0 when the Middlesex offense suddenly got up a head of steam.
On a crucial fourth-down-and-inches, the Middlesex coach was certain his team had enough momentum to easily get the first down. The offense stepped
up to the line, but before the ball could be snapped, the lights went off! The game had to be halted.

For 15 minutes the stadium remained dark, while the players waited. When the lights finally came back on, the momentum had shifted. The Middlesex offense ran its play but came up short on its attempt to make a first down. Roselle Park took over the ball and went on to win the game 19–0. Talk about a dark victory!

GOALPOST PUNCH

Ohio State met the University of Alabama in the 1978 Sugar Bowl. Ohio State was guided by the great but temperamental coach Woody Hayes. By the end of the first half Alabama was way out in front of Ohio State, and Woody's temper was almost out of control. As Hayes walked to the locker room at half time, he kept his head down and didn't watch where he was going. Thunk! Woody bumped right into the goalpost by accident. Hayes angrily jumped back, glared at the goalpost blocking his path, and then punched the metal pole.

BROWN OUT

The Cleveland Browns of the NFL were founded by and named for their coach, Paul Brown. The team's greatest player ever was a running back named Jim Brown. It seems that Cleveland has a knack for attracting football personnel with the last name of Brown. From 1957 to 1980, Cleveland had seven players on its roster with the last name Brown, and during that same span, the Browns were without a player named Brown for a total of only four years.

TROJAN WAR

Mike Price tried a wacky way to psyche up his Washington State Cougars football team for a game against the University of Southern California Trojans in 1989. Coach Price hired an actor dressed up as the USC Trojan mascot to gallop onto the WSU practice field on a white horse. When the Trojan warrior appeared, Mike Price took out a starter's pistol loaded with blanks and fired shots at the actor until he slumped in the saddle and rode off the field mortally wounded! Unfortunately, Price's stunt didn't work. USC ended up beating Washington, 18–17.

BAD SIGN

Northwestern University has struggled through some dark days on the gridiron. In the early 1980's the Wildcats established an unwanted record by losing over 30 games in a row.

Of course, Northwestern's losing streak was the target of many jokes and gags. When Doug Single, the Wildcats' athletic director, first drove to the school to be interviewed for the job, he saw a strange road sign on the way to the Northwestern campus. The sign read: INTERSTATE 94. Under it someone had printed the words: "NORTHWESTERN 0!"

Now that's a funny football sense of humor!

MARSHALL MISHAP

All-Pro defensive end Jim Marshall had a remarkable, injury-free NFL career that spanned 20 seasons. Marshall set a pro record by starting 282 consecutive games for the Minnesota Vikings. It was amazing that Jim was never sidelined by any bumps or bruises.

In 1980, the year after Jim Marshall had retired from the rough-and-tumble world of the NFL, he took up a new hobby: hang gliding. That year, unfortunately, Jim injured himself when his hang glider crashed into a light pole at a high school athletic field.

TWO-HEADED QUARTERBACK

In 1956, the New York Giants had two outstanding quarterbacks on their roster. Charlie Conerly was a great athlete who could throw a football the entire length of the field. Don Heinrich wasn't as physically gifted as Conerly, but had a great mind for the strategy of the game. Heinrich could read opposing defenses extremely well and quickly formulate a plan of attack for the Giants' offense.

To best utilize both quarterbacks, the Giants' coaching staff came up with a unique but strange solution. Don Heinrich would start each game and play several series to figure out the defense's weaknesses. Then Conerly would enter the game, and Heinrich would tell him which plays would work and how to attack the opposition. Heinrich would sit out the rest of the game, acting as an advisor to the offense. It was almost as if the Giants were using one man's brain to help run another man's body!

The Giants' two-headed quarterback system worked well that year—New York went on to become the champions of the NFL!

YIPES!

One of the strangest college football games in history was played in 1980 between Oregon's Portland State University and Delaware State College. Portland State had future NFL star Neil Lomax at quarterback, and the outcome of the game was just a bit lopsided in Portland's favor. Portland State defeated Delaware State by the unbelievable score of 105–0.

ALL-AMERICAN MESS-UPS

Don't believe everything you read in the newspapers. In 1978, United Press International named offensive center Brent Boyd of UCLA to the first team of its All-American football squad. Boyd was a good player, but there was a slight problem.
He had been injured in 1978 and did not play in a single game the entire season. When UPI discovered its mistake, it dropped Boyd from its All-American team.

In 1982, tackle Jimbo Covert of the University of Pittsburgh had a similar problem with the Associated Press All-American college football team. Covert was left off the squad by mistake, even though sportswriters had voted him in as their second-team selection. That mistake was also corrected. Covert was eventually added to the team.

HOSPITAL HELP

Despite being confined to a hospital bed after undergoing an appendectomy, San Francisco 49ers defensive secondary coach Ray Rhodes still took part in his team's win over the New York Giants in 1990.
Rhodes coached the 49ers secondary from his hospital room using a special telephone hookup to the playing field. Rhodes watched the game  on TV and phoned comments to players on the sidelines. They relayed his wishes out onto the field using hand signals.

IRISH LUCK

The University of Oklahoma took on the University of Notre Dame at the start of the 1953 college football season. Notre Dame won that game, giving Oklahoma an 0–1 record. However, Oklahoma didn't get discouraged. In fact, it spurred them on to victory. The Sooners went on to set a Division 1 college record by winning their next 47 games in a row! The Oklahoma team did not lose or tie another football game until 1957. And which team do you think ended the Oklahoma streak that year? Notre Dame, of course!

WALKIE-TALKIE TALK

When the great Paul Brown was coach of the Cleveland Browns, he began using a walkie-talkie to call plays for his quarterback from the sidelines. After a few games of Brown's walkie-talkie coaching, the National Football League outlawed his idea.

FOOTBALL FOLLY

T here have been a lot of lopsided football scores in the history of the sport. However, it's unlikely that any gridiron team will ever endure a worse defeat than tiny Cumberland College suffered at the hands of powerful Georgia Tech on October 7, 1916 at Grant Field in Atlanta. On that day the "Rambling Wreck" from Georgia Tech, coached by football immortal John Heisman (for whom the Heisman Trophy is named), chalked up the most points ever scored in a single football game. Georgia Tech outplayed little Cumberland from the opening whistle and led 126–0 at halftime. And things didn't get any better for Cumberland after that. They ended up losing to Georgia Tech by the score of 222–0! And interestingly enough, neither school made a first down in the game—Georgia Tech scored every time it touched the ball!

SCORING MACHINE

T alk about a high-powered offense! In 1922, Jersey Shore High School of Pennsylvania had a pretty good offensive scoring machine. The school racked up an astounding total of 676 points in just nine games that season. That's an average of 75.1 points per game, which is still a record!

LONGTIME COACH

In 1892, the University of Chicago launched its football program by hiring Amos Alonzo Stagg as its gridiron coach. Stagg coached the University of Chicago team for an amazing 41 consecutive years. Finally he was asked to retire as Chicago's coach. Stagg left the job but refused to retire. He went on to coach several other college football teams, and remained a gridiron mentor until he was in his nineties. Stagg's career as a college coach was the longest in football history!

WHOOPS!

At a pro football game in New Orleans in 1978, a fan in the stands became so mad over a call against his team that he threw his binoculars at the referee. But he missed the referee and hit a police officer instead!

A PLANE FACT—MONEY TALKS!

The University of Nebraska Cornhuskers were scheduled to meet the University of Miami Hurricanes in a New York bowl game in 1962 known as the Gotham Bowl. However, Nebraska's chancellor, Clifford Hardin, had doubts about the Gotham Bowl's ability to pay the Cornhuskers' $35,000 appearance guarantee. When the Nebraska team boarded a plane in Lincoln, Nebraska for their flight to New York, Hardin refused to allow the plane to take off until Gotham Bowl officials delivered $35,000 in certified checks to Nebraska officials already in New York. After some tense waiting, the money was delivered and the plane took off. Nebraska ended up winning the game, 36–34, but the Gotham Bowl never did make enough money to survive. Luckily for the Cornhuskers, they got paid in advance!

POINTLESS RUNNING

Baltimore Colts running back Joe Washington had a good year—but not a great year—in 1978. Washington carried the ball 240 times for the Colts that season, but didn't score a single touchdown! However, he did throw one touchdown pass on an option play.

HAVE A SEAT

Q uarterback Cliff Stoudt had a strange start in his NFL career. Stoudt joined the Pittsburgh Steelers in 1977 as the backup quarterback to Terry Bradshaw. As Bradshaw's sub, Stoudt got plenty of rest. He sat on the bench for 56 straight games without ever getting the opportunity to play in an NFL contest. Finally in 1980, Stoudt got a chance to get into a game, and he logged some playing time against the Chicago Bears.

FINE WITH ME

S t. Louis Cardinals receiver Dave Stief was really excited when he caught a touchdown pass against the Detroit Lions in a game in 1978. Instead of giving the ball back to the official, he fired it up at the broadcasters' booth as a joke. NFL officials didn't think Dave's stunt was so funny. He ended up getting fined for losing the ball.

HAND-ME-DOWNS

In 1979, George Washington (New York) High
School's football team had one tough week.
First, all of the team's football uniforms were stolen
from their locker room. Then, to avoid having to
cancel the next game on their schedule, the squad had
to wear borrowed uniforms from two neighboring
schools. Worst of all, they ended up losing the game
they played in their borrowed uniforms!

LONG BOMB?

Football is a sport where players sometimes throw
the long bomb. In November 1991, however,
high school football players in Massachusetts were
more concerned about a bomb of a different kind. It
was a real bomb, and it was buried under the fifty-
yard line of Wellesley High School's football field!
The bomb was discovered by a janitor two days
before the Wellesley High School Raiders took on the
Needham High School Rockets in the 104th meeting
between the two rivals. Police were notified, and the
bomb was removed and exploded. The game was

played as
scheduled, but
how the bomb
got on the field
remained a
mystery. By the
way, Wellesley
defeated
Needham 35–7
in the contest.

JET LAG

In 1978 the University of Wyoming played the University of Hawaii. The Wyoming team flew 5,000 miles to Honolulu on the day of the scheduled night game with Hawaii's Rainbow Warriors. Wyoming took an early lead in the game, but lagged behind in the end and lost, 27–22.

FOR MEN ONLY?

If you think you have to be a tough guy to play football, you may be out of touch with the times. One of the best high school football guards in southern California in 1991 was a 5' 6", 140-pound senior girl named Rebecca Andreas. Rebecca played for Lee Vining High School in 1990 and 1991 and was voted a member of the All-League team.

JUST FOR KICKS

Though the New Orleans Saints were a big underdog when they took on the powerful Detroit Lions on November 8, 1970, the Lions held only a 17–16 lead with 11 seconds to play in the game. The Saints had the ball on their own 37-yard line. They needed a seemingly impossible field goal—more than 60 yards long—to win. No one in NFL history had ever kicked one that far. Nevertheless, onto the field trotted New Orleans' kicker Tom Dempsey to attempt the game-winning boot. The ball was snapped and Dempsey amazed the world by kicking a 63-yard field goal to win the contest. It was the longest field goal in NFL history. What makes it even more astonishing is that the man who kicked it had been born with a handicap. Dempsey was born without a right hand and only part of the right foot he used for kicking. To kick, Dempsey wore an artificial right foot encased in a specially designed football shoe. Yet despite his handicap, Tom Dempsey kicked the longest NFL field goal ever.

WHAT SPORTSMANSHIP?

There's nothing like good sportsmanship on the gridiron. But someone apparently forgot to tell that to the players on the University of Wyoming and the Colorado State football teams in 1978. That year, several members of the two teams got into a fistfight during the coin toss—before the game had even begun!

WHAT A SCHEDULE

The Sewanee (Tennessee) football team had quite a gridiron schedule in 1899. Sewanee (now called the University of the South) played five games in five different cities against five powerful college football teams all in a matter of six days. First on the list was the unbeaten University of Texas. Sewanee beat Texas 12–0. The next day Sewanee played and beat Texas A&M 10–0. On the third day Sewanee took on Tulane University and throttled them 23–0. After their first three wins, Sewanee took Sunday off to rest before continuing its schedule. On Monday Sewanee met and defeated Louisiana State 34–0. The team finished its road trip the next day with a 12–0 win over Mississippi State. In just six days a football team from tiny Sewanee had chalked up victories over five big-time football opponents!

AMAZING, BUT NOT OFFICIAL

Montana State University's freshman football team took on a team from Billings Polytech on November 1, 1924. Kicking for Montana State that day was Forest Peters, and he was a busy man. During the course of the game, Peters attempted an amazing 22 field goals, and made 17 of them. Unfortunately, since the game wasn't in varsity competition, it didn't count as a record!

GAME INSURANCE

All-American running back Herschel Walker of Georgia saw a bright future for himself as an NFL player if he could avoid injuries. Just to be on the safe side, Walker took out a reported one-million-dollar, one-year insurance policy on himself with Lloyds of London in 1981.

BUSY DAY

Running back Gil Fenerty of Holy Cross had a busy day in a college football game against Columbia University in October 1983. Fenerty, who played only slightly more than half of the game, rushed for 337 yards and six touchdowns!

KICKED OUT

In 1978 the Philadelphia Eagles couldn't decide who their punter should be. The Eagles sometimes used punter Mitch Hoopes and other times used punter Rick Engles. Apparently unable to make up their minds, Philadelphia hired and fired both Mitch Hoopes and Rick Engles *three times each* that season!

HOW WAS THE TRIP?

The University of Nebraska football team played the University of Hawaii in December 1976. To get to the game, the Cornhuskers football team had to travel about 4,000 miles by plane. Of course, the Nebraska team didn't go to the game alone. Some 16,000 loyal Nebraska fans went to the game on numerous chartered jets. In all, the trip cost the Cornhuskers' fans and supporters about ten million dollars!

STOP THIEF

The Michigan Wolverines were excited about playing in the 1978 Rose Bowl. But they had bad luck before the game could be played. Thieves broke into the gym where Michigan was practicing prior to the big game, and stole $2,700 worth of the Wolverines' equipment, including game jerseys, pants, helmets, and shoes.

TO COIN A PHRASE

Years ago the Washington Redskins were known as the Boston Redskins and were coached by a man named Lone Star Dietz. Dietz was a witty man with a great sense of humor who never had much luck as a coach. Once when the Red- skins were playing the New York

Giants, Dietz met with his captains on the field. "If we win the toss, choose to kick off to the Giants," Dietz said. The captains nodded as Dietz left the field to go through a long tunnel that led up to a coaches' observation booth high in the stands. Just as he entered the tunnel, the Redskins coach heard that his team had won the toss. But by the time he reached the observation booth he saw the Redskins on the field lined up to receive the kickoff. Dietz angrily picked up the telephone that connected him with the field. "What's going on?" Dietz grumbled to an assistant coach. "I told those guys to kick off if we won the toss."

"We did coach," the assistant quickly explained. "The score is now 7–0." Much to Dietz's chagrin, the Giants had run the opening kickoff back for a touchdown!

HATS OFF

The great Curly Lambeau, who coached the Green Bay Packers for many years, was a bit superstitious. He believed it was bad luck for him or anyone on his team to wear the same hat to more than one game. That superstition was never a problem for Curly. He had a habit of getting over-excited during football games and tearing up whatever he happened to be wearing at the time.

THE REF CAN'T COUNT

The Dallas Cowboys and the Detroit Lions were matched up in a touch football contest on November 15, 1981. With time running out, the score was deadlocked at 24–24. Onto the field trotted Lions' kicker Eddie Murray for a last-second field goal attempt. The kick was good! Detroit won the game 27–24, but Dallas felt cheated. In fact, Dallas *was* cheated. Film of the game-winning goal revealed that the Lions had 12 men on the field instead of the legal number of 11. Unfortunately, the officials never counted the Lions' players, and Detroit ended up the victor.

QUICK KICKER

In a 1923 game between Rutgers and Villanova, kicker Homer Hazel scored a touchdown only eight seconds after the game had begun. His opening kickoff sailed into the end zone, where a Villanova player attempted to receive the ball. Unfortunately, he fumbled it. Hazel, who happened to be a very fast runner, raced down the field and recovered the ball in the end zone while it was still in play. Touchdown, Rutgers!

FUMBLING FOR A CALL

One of the funniest fumble decisions ever made in college football happened when Paul "Bear" Bryant was the coach of the University of Kentucky many years ago. Kentucky was playing the University of Tennessee. The ball was fumbled near the Kentucky bench. As people on the sidelines scrambled out of the way, a large box filled with footballs was knocked over and eight footballs rolled out onto the field. Counting the game ball, that made nine footballs—all of which were recovered by players on the field! Since the officials couldn't tell which ball was the game ball, they were faced with a real dilemma. Finally the referee awarded possession of the ball to Tennessee, because Tennessee players had recovered five of the nine footballs, while Kentucky players had only recovered four!

NOT OLD, JUST EXPERIENCED

Luke Phillups, the football coach at Monterey Peninsula College in 1980, never discouraged any player from trying out for his team. However, when Fritz von Berg signed up for the squad, Coach Phillups was a bit worried. Von Berg was a fifty-year-old student who had last played football in the army way back in 1949. Despite his age, von Berg passed all of his physical tests and became a member of his college football team that season. He even played in a few games!

TO PLAY OR NOT TO PLAY

The Pittsburgh Steelers signed a former Notre Dame player with a very famous name in 1934. However, that ex-member of the Fighting Irish didn't have a famous football name. The player's name was William Shakespeare!

TRAP PLAY

Dick Vermeil was one of the NFL's most intense coaches. He lived and breathed football. In 1980 Vermeil was out playing golf with a friend when he hit his ball into a sand trap. Dick stayed in the trap a long time, which puzzled his friend. Suddenly, Vermeil became very excited and shouted for his friend to join him in the sand trap. When Vermeil's partner looked in the trap, he saw X's and O's written in the sand. "Do you think this will work?" Dick asked his buddy. Vermeil had scratched out a football play in the sand with his golf club.

LAST BUT BEST

In 1975 the Balboa Boat Club of Newport Beach, California started a strange football tradition. The club awards the special Lowsman Trophy to a college football player every year. The trophy is handed out to the very last college football player selected in the National Football League's annual draft.

The winner of the Lowsman Trophy is given a banquet in his honor, has a horse race and a regatta named after him, and is awarded the trophy and other gifts. Winning the award is a strange honor to say the least. The trophy is of a football player reaching for a football he just dropped!

FIRST-RATE FOOTBALL

In 1980 everyone who visited Chicago was interested in how the Chicago Bears had fared in their game the week before. That was because the McCormick Inn, a huge hotel in Chicago, offered various deductions on room rates depending on the Bears' performance. If the Bears won their game, there was an automatic $3.00 deduction in the rate. An additional $1.00 was also deducted every time any Bear player scored more than one touchdown. Another $1.00 was deducted from the rate every time a Bear player threw a touchdown pass. In fact, there were all kinds of ways to get reduced room rates at the McCormick whenever the Bears won a game. It was no wonder most visitors to Chicago in 1980 became instant Bear fans.

SOCK IT TO ME?

In 1980 linebacker Reggie Williams of the Cincinnati Bengals learned that the NFL is tough when it comes to enforcing its dress code. In a game against the Houston Oilers, Williams didn't tape his socks tightly enough around his legs and they fell down during the contest. After the game the NFL fined Williams $1,000 for having "droopy socks" while playing in an NFL game.

PUNCH ANYONE?

Linebacker Bob Crable of Notre Dame was known as a tough player. In fact, in the late 1970's, Crable psyched himself up for a game against the University of Southern California in a strange way. Bob taped a photo of USC's great running back Charles White to the wall of his dorm room. Every time Crable walked past the photo he punched it. By the time Notre Dame was ready to play USC, Bob Crable had punched a huge hole in his wall!

OLD GUY

William Walter "Pudge" Heffelfinger was a member of the legendary, undefeated Yale team of 1888. An All-American at Yale, Pudge was voted into College Football's Hall of Fame. Heffelfinger never stopped loving football no matter how old he was. He once played in a game against the Ohio State All-Stars when he was 55 years old. Ten years later, Pudge was at it again. He played in a high school alumni football game in St. Paul, Minnesota when he was 65 years old!

NOT FLOWER POWER

The University of Illinois was scheduled to play UCLA in the 1984 Rose Bowl at Pasadena, California. However, fans in the stadium weren't sure just who was playing in the contest when the electronic scoreboard lit up just before the big game. The night before the Rose Bowl clash, two students from Cal Tech managed to sneak into the stadium and reprogram the electric junction box so the teams listed on the scoreboard read "Cal Tech" and Cal Tech's academic rival "MIT," instead of Illinois and UCLA. The fans in the stands thought the prank was funny, but Rose Bowl officials didn't. The two Cal Tech students were charged with malicious mischief and trespassing!

BIG MISTAKE

In 1926 the University of Notre Dame football team was undefeated and highly ranked in the country. With eight victories already under their belt, the Fighting Irish weren't worried about playing tiny Carnegie Tech of Pennsylvania—the next team on their schedule. Knute Rockne, the Notre Dame coach, was more concerned about Army, the team Notre Dame would meet after Carnegie Tech. Rockne felt Carnegie Tech would pose no problem at all to his mighty Fighting Irish, so he decided not even to attend the game. Knute left the squad in the hands of assistant coach Hank Anderson while he traveled to Chicago to scout the Army-Navy game. Unfortunately for Notre Dame, someone forgot to tell little Carnegie Tech they were supposed to lose. Tech took on mighty Notre Dame in Pittsburgh on November 27, 1926 and—you guessed it—walloped the Irish 19– 0, to end Notre Dame's hopes of an undefeated season. Of course, the person most upset by Notre Dame's stunning defeat was a guy in Chicago named Knute Rockne!

BIG MONEY

The first pro-football world championship was played in 1933 between the Chicago Bears and the New York Giants. It wasn't exactly the big-money game it is today. Each winning player on the championship team received $210.34, while the losers were paid $140.22 each.

SHORT STUFF

Dallas Cowboys' quarterback Eddie LeBaron was one of the shortest quarterbacks ever to play in the NFL. LeBaron was only 5' 7" tall when he played for the Cowboys in the early 60's. LeBaron also threw one of the shortest unofficial touchdown passes ever. On October 9, 1960 the Cowboys were playing the Washington Redskins, and Dallas had the ball about two inches from the Washington end zone. The defense was expecting the Cowboys to run, but LeBaron caught everyone off guard by tossing a touchdown pass to Dick Bielski. Little Eddie LeBaron's mini-touchdown flip to Bielski may be the shortest scoring toss in NFL history.

RAINING FOOTBALLS

When the University of Pittsburgh took on Florida State University in Florida in 1982, both teams used some slick football plays. That was because the game was played in a driving rainstorm. The rain was so bad it affected the performance of Florida's punter, Kelly Lowrey. Lowrey tried to punt a wet ball and slipped. He ended up kicking the ball into the back of one of his linemen. The pigskin bounced into the air and landed in the arms of a Pittsburgh defender, who grabbed it and ran for a touchdown. Pittsburgh won the game 31–17.

PLUM CRAZY

One of the wackiest pass plays in NFL history occurred in a game between the Cleveland Browns and the Chicago Cardinals in 1959. At quarterback for the Browns was Milt Plum. During the game, Plum dropped back to pass. As he threw the ball, a Chicago defender blocked the pass. The ball bounced back to Plum, who caught it and then raced forward for a 20-yard pickup! Strange as it sounds, the play went down in the record book as a Milt Plum to Milt Plum completed pass for a 20-yard gain.

TIMBER!

The New York Giants suffered a weird defeat at the hands of the Los Angeles Rams in September 1984. In that game the Rams scored three safeties, blocked two punts, and sacked the Giants' quarterback a total of five times. The Giants added to the unusual sequence of events by missing two extra points and giving up an 83-yard punt return for a touchdown. However, the oddest moment in that strange contest came when the goalpost uprights at one end of the field suddenly toppled over for no apparent reason! The game had to be delayed ten minutes while the lopsided goalpost was repaired.

A ROSE IS A ROSE

The 1939 Rose Bowl was the scene of a series of strange events. Unbeaten, untied, and unscored-upon Duke University was leading the underdog University of Southern California Trojans 3– 0 with minutes to go in the game. Up in the Trojan press box was a young coach named Joe Wilensky. Wilensky's job was to relay instructions from the USC varsity coaches by telephone to head

coach Howard Jones on the field. Since there were only minutes to go, the varsity coaches left the press box, leaving Wilensky alone. Then Wilensky had an idea. Pretending he had instructions from the varsity coaches, he told Coach Jones to put in Doyle Nave and Al Kruger. Nave was only a fourth-string quarterback and Kruger was a substitute receiver. Listening to what he thought was advice from his assistants, head coach Jones put the two subs into the Rose Bowl, even though they'd hardly played during the regular season!

Amazingly the Nave-to-Kruger combination clicked like magic. Doyle Nave completed pass after pass to Al Kruger. USC marched down the field and scored just before time expired! The two sub players became heroes. USC scored the first points against Duke that season and beat Duke 7–3. Yet the strange events of the day didn't end there. After the game Nave and Kruger were late getting out of the locker room. The team bus left without them and they had to walk back to their hotel!

LONG GAME

When NCAA Division 1-AA football teams made a rule in 1981 that tied games should continue into an overtime period to determine a winner, they didn't know what they were getting into. In September 1982 the University of Maine and the University of Rhode Island ended up tied 21–21 at the end of four quarters of play. The teams then continued to play in overtime, with each side alternating ball possession and matching scores. The first team that could not score during its possession would lose the game. The result was a game that lasted 3 hours, 46 minutes! Rhode Island finally emerged a 58–55 victor over Maine, but not before the longest game in college-football history had been played.

HUT! HUT! HUT!

Russ Washington, who played offensive tackle for the San Diego Chargers in the 1970's, was a hard person to contact in the off-season. Washington made his off-season home on a small island in the Pacific Ocean and lived in a grass hut!

THE RIGHT MAN

The Northern Arizona University football team got a new head coach in 1989. And all things considered, you'd have to say the university picked the right person for the job. Northern Arizona's nickname is the Lumberjacks. The head coach they hired was named Steve Axman.

IT'S HOW YOU PLAY THE GAME

A lot of coaches say it's not whether you win or lose that counts, but how you play the game. That may be true, but a win every now and then is still nice. For the Iberia (Missouri) High School football teams of the late 1960's and early 1970's, however, even one win was asking too much. Iberia's gridiron squads lost a national record 72 football games in a row from 1965 to 1974.

Iberia's record was in jeopardy in 1986. Glenville High School of Minnesota had lost 70 football games in a row when it took on Ellendale-Geneva High School in September 1986. Luckily, Glenville won the contest 14–8 to end its eight-year losing streak.

HANDS OFF, DUDE

High schools in Tucson, Arizona used to have a nice, friendly football tradition. After each and every game, the teams would line up and shake hands. But in the middle of the 1980 season that tradition went right out the window. It all happened on Halloween night. Paloverde High School met Pueblo High in a gridiron contest. When the game was over, Paloverde had ended their 21-game losing streak by beating heavily favored Pueblo. Tempers flared. The teams lined up but the players didn't shake hands. Instead they started whacking each other with their helmets! A brawl started that involved players, students, and fans. After the fight, Tucson's district athletic director made a new rule. Teams were ordered *not* to shake hands after football games. Later in the season the rule was changed, allowing coaches to decide if their teams should or should not shake hands after a game. In 1980, to shake or not to shake sure was the question when it came to high-school football in Tucson, Arizona.

NOW YOU SEE IT, NOW YOU DON'T

Little St. Peter's High of New Jersey was outmatched when they took on powerful Franklin Township High School in 1965. Since St. Pete's couldn't run or pass well against Franklin, they resorted to trickery. After a touchdown, Franklin kicked off. As soon as the St. Peter's player fielded the ball, he hunched over to hide it. He was quickly joined by all ten members of his team. They huddled around him and hunched over as if they too had the ball. Then the St. Peter's players suddenly broke the huddle and started to run down the field in a hunched-over position! It was difficult to tell exactly who had the ball. Unfortunately, the crazy trick play looked good but didn't work. The real ball carrier was tackled by a Franklin defender after only a modest gain.

A REAL HOT DOG

Some pro football players are hungry for victory. Others are money hungry. During a preseason game in the 1970's, Ezra Johnson of the Green Bay Packers was just plain hungry. While his teammates were out on the field, Johnson accepted a hot dog offered to him by a fan and munched on it while standing on the sidelines.

BAG MAN

The New Orleans Saints of the NFL had some tough years in the 1970's and early 1980's. In fact, up to and including 1980, the Saints had never had a winning season in their 14-year history. Unfortunately, the 1980 season was a total disaster, with the Saints losing their first 12 games in a row! New Orleans fans wanted to support their team, but many were embarrassed to be seen at the Saints' games. So what did the fans do? They began showing up at New Orleans' games wearing paper bags over their heads with slits cut out for their eyes!

A PAIR OF WINNERS

There have been many Heisman Trophy winners since it was first awarded in 1935. However, in all those years, only once have two Heisman winners played for the same college team at the same time. Those two winners were teammates Glenn Davis and Doc Blanchard, who played for Army in the mid-1940's. Blanchard won the Heisman in 1945, their junior year, and Davis won it in 1946, their senior year.

KICKING YOURSELF

Texas A&M kicked itself right out of the game when it played Southern Methodist University in 1980. SMU scored its first points of the contest when linebacker Byron Hunt blocked an A&M punt, grabbed the ball, and ran for a touchdown. Minutes later A&M punted again. This time, SMU's John Simmons fielded the ball and ran 66 yards for a score. Later in the game, Simmons returned another punt 53 yards, which led to an SMU field goal. If that wasn't enough, John Simmons later blocked a Texas A&M field-goal attempt. Byron Hunt picked up the ball and ran 51 yards, which led to another SMU field goal. Texas A&M didn't get a kick out of this game. SMU eventually won it 27–0.

WHAT A THROW!

If you can't complete passes, you can't play quarterback in the NFL. On September 24, 1950, quarterback Jim Hardy of the Chicago Cardinals completed a lot of passes, but that didn't prove much about his NFL quarterbacking ability.

Playing against the Philadelphia Eagles that day, Hardy attempted 39 passes and threw 8 interceptions to Eagles' defenders. Jim Hardy completed more than one in every five passes he tossed to the opposing team! That's still the NFL record for most passes intercepted in a game.

WRONG WAY— RIGHT PLAY

The play Coach Dave Herbert called sounded crazy and looked worse, but it ended up being the right call in a high school football game in Falkner, Mississippi in 1988. Herbert's team from Tishomingo High School was beating Falkner High 16–14 late in the game when Coach Herbert called time. Even though Tishomingo had the ball and was leading the game with only seven seconds left, the team was in trouble—in order to qualify for the state play-offs, Tishomingo had to win this game by four or more points. Because it was too far away for a field-goal attempt, Dave Herbert quickly concocted a wild plan. He told his quarterback, who happened to be his son, to take the ball and run fifty-five yards backwards into his own end zone for a safety, which would tie the score!

The quarterback couldn't believe his ears but nevertheless obeyed. Tishomingo gave up a safety, and the game was tied at the end of regulation play. Since high school games in Mississippi are settled in an overtime period, the teams continued to play. Sure enough, Tishomingo went on to defeat Falkner 22–16. The six-point margin of victory sent Coach Dave Herbert's team into the play-offs. And it all happened because of a crazy wrong-way play!

BEST FOR LAST

Pat Stoqua played for the Ottawa Rough Riders of the Canadian Football League in 1981 and didn't catch a single touchdown pass the entire regular season. However, his effort in the CFL playoffs ended up sending Ottawa into Canada's championship game against the Edmonton Eskimos. In the Rough Riders' playoff game against the Hamilton Tiger-Cats, Stoqua snared his first touchdown pass of the year. It was a 102-yard scoring pass (fields in Canada are 120 yards long). Ottawa won the game, 17–13!

MONEY MAN

In the 1970's the University of Alabama football squad coached by Paul "Bear" Bryant was the team every Southern school loved to beat. Alabama was so good in those days that fans from other schools would do just about anything to try to insure a victory over Bryant's Crimson Tide. In one game, Alabama was beating Auburn when an Auburn player named Strickland blocked two punts to help give Auburn a 17–16 win. When the gun sounded, grateful Auburn fans jumped out of the stands and began to shove money into Strickland's jersey as a reward for his efforts. Stories say that by the time Strickland reached the locker room he was almost $5,000 richer!

TIGER TALE

Princeton Tiger football fans pulled a sneaky stunt before the 1946 Princeton–Yale football game. Before the game was played, Princeton supporters sneaked into the Yale Bowl and burned a huge letter "P" right in the middle of the Bulldogs' football field.

ROSY RECORD

The University of Michigan was a gridiron dynamo in 1901. The Wolverines, coached by Fielding Yost, pulverized every team on their schedule that year en route to a perfect 10–0 record. Michigan was so good that season that they scored 550 points on offense while giving up 0 points on defense!

The most lopsided victory the Wolverines notched that year was a big win over the University of Buffalo (New York). Michigan won the game by the incredible score of 128–0.

At the end of the regular season, Stanford University challenged Michigan to play in a special game on January 1, 1902. The game was held in Pasadena, California, and Michigan won it 49–0. That game in 1902 started a long tradition known as the Rose Bowl.

IF YOU CAN'T BE GOOD— BE LUCKY!

To get into the play-offs, a professional football team usually has to have a pretty good record. That wasn't the case in 1981 when the Montreal Alouettes made the Canadian Football League play-offs. Montreal sneaked into the Eastern Division's third play-off berth behind the Hamilton Tiger-Cats and the Ottawa Rough Riders with an anemic record of only 3 wins and 13 losses. The Montreal record was the worst ever for a CFL play-off qualifier. However, it was better than the 2–14 record of the Toronto Argonauts, who finished behind them in the four-team conference.

GUIDO OF ALL TRADES

Guido Merkens had an unusual football career. In 1978 Merkens started his pro career with the Houston Oilers as a defensive cornerback. When the Oilers needed receiver help, Guido was switched to wide receiver. And when Merkens returned to the Oilers in 1979 he became a quarterback. In a single year Guido Merkens played three very different positions in the NFL!

FOOTBALL TWEET

im Rossovich was one of the NFL's zaniest players. Rossovich played linebacker and defensive end for both the Philadelphia Eagles and the Houston Oilers. Once while sitting at a team meeting with the Eagles, Rossovich opened his mouth wide, and out flew a tiny sparrow!

LIKE FATHER, LIKE SON

ierce Frauenheim had a successful career as a football coach at Immaculata High School in New Jersey. Under Frauenheim's guidance, the Immaculata Spartans won several state titles. All of that success obviously had a big influence on Pierce's sons. In 1991 three of them decided to become high school football coaches. That season, Pierce, Jr., David, and Michael Frauenheim were all named assistant coaches to their father at Immaculata High School. Now that's keeping coaching in the family!

FIELD DAY

Almost all football fans know that a football playing field is 100 yards long from goal line to goal line and 50 yards wide. However, the field wasn't always that size. In 1869 a regulation football field measured 360 yards long and 225 yards wide! When the first Intercollegiate Football Association was formed in 1880, the size was reduced to 110 yards long and 53 yards wide. The size of a football field took on its modern dimensions in 1912.

WET HEAD

Prankster Fred Smerlas used to pull his favorite joke over and over again on his fellow Buffalo Bills players. Smerlas always got a big laugh out of filling up players' helmets with shaving cream!

TAKE A DIVE

Halfback Bob Fenimore of Oklahoma A&M was one happy ball carrier when he broke away from Texas Tech defenders in a night game played on October 7, 1944. Fenimore scooted down the field for a big gainer that looked like it would result in a sure touchdown. He was headed for the goal line when a Texas Tech tackler started to close in on him from behind. Fenimore realized he'd have to dive into the end zone to escape. Bob leaped into the air and crossed what he thought was the goal line.

Unfortunately, Fenimore had miscalculated where he was on the field. What he actually did was dive across the 10-yard line, landing ten yards short of the end zone!

SCHOOL SPIRIT

In 1980 Hannan High School in West Virginia didn't have a big-time football program. In fact, Hannan, a small school with only 250 students in grades 7 through 12, had only 60 boys in the upper grades eligible to play football that year.

Nevertheless, the small enrollment didn't stop the school from playing a ten-game varsity football schedule. Hannan High opened its season with only 19 players on its roster. After a few injuries, the team played several games with only 11 players healthy enough to participate. At other times during the season, Hannan used two 95-pound freshmen as starters. Hannan High School didn't win any of the ten games on their schedule that season, but they sure were victors when it came to courage and determination!

NO THANKS

Preston Pearson played running back for the Dallas Cowboys in the 1978 season. In that season's Super Bowl, the Cowboys lost to the Pittsburgh Steelers. After the game Pearson returned to Pittsburgh, where he lived with his wife Linda in the off-season. Pearson gave his wife his Super Bowl check to deposit, and she took it to the local bank. When the bank teller saw the check he said, "Mrs. Pearson, I'm not sure you'd be interested, but for a deposit of this size you qualify for our free gift—a record album featuring a review of the Steelers' season and their fight song." Since the Steelers had beaten her husband's team in the Super Bowl, Linda Pearson politely declined the offer.

EVEN STEVEN

In 1932 the Green Bay Packers met the Chicago Bears in a tough National Football League contest. The game turned into a rough-and-tumble defensive battle. As time wore on, neither team could score. Finally the Packers tackled a Bears' ball carrier in the end zone for a two-point safety. The two points proved to be enough, as the Packers edged the Bears by that slim score to win the game.

In 1938 the two teams met in another great defensive struggle. Once again the game was determined by a mere two-point safety. But this time the Bears beat the Packers by the score of 2–0!

JUMP BALL

There is nothing strange about blocking a field-goal attempt. But the way R.C. Owens of the Baltimore Colts once blocked a field goal against the Washington Redskins was definitely unusual. Owens, who played pro football during the 1960's, had been a great basketball player in college, and he could really leap. In a game against Washington, Owens put his jumping ability to the test. As Bob Khayat of the Redskins attempted a field goal, Owens backed up into his end zone and stood near the goal posts. The ball was kicked. As it sailed toward the goal-post it started to descend. It looked like the kick would just clear the crossbar. However, at exactly the right moment, Owens leaped high into the air and tipped the ball away, blocking the field-goal attempt. It was one of the strangest blocks of a kick in football history!

NOT A BAD PAIR

Quarterback Joe Theismann, who won a Super Bowl with the Washington Redskins, and receiver Drew Pearson, who won a Super Bowl with the Dallas Cowboys, both went to the same high school in New Jersey. In fact, the two Super Bowl stars were teammates at South River High School, where Drew was the back-up quarterback to Joe!

NUT CASE

Gil Dobie was one of the greatest college football coaches in history. But he was also a big grouch. Dobie could win games but not the hearts of his players or the fans. He was so grumpy that he was nicknamed "Gloomy Gil." Dobie coached the University of Washington from 1908 to 1916 and his team never lost a single game. Normally that would endear a coach to the fans. But Gloomy Gil was so despised that fans in Washington not only booed him constantly but also pelted him with peanuts from the stands every time they got the chance. Eventually Dobie left Washington and took over the coaching reins first at Navy and then at Cornell. At Cornell he was also successful—and just as unpopular. But at least at Cornell they didn't throw things at him.

LOW NUMBER

In 1930 the maximum number of players allowed on a National Football League team was only 20. Some teams had only 16 players on their rosters, which was the league minimum. Can you imagine a modern NFL team trying to get through a season with only 16 players on its roster?

A LACK OF PEP

Coach Dana Bible of the University of Nebraska gave one of college football's most original halftime talks in 1936. At the time, his Nebraska gridiron squad was losing 9–0 to Indiana University. Coach Bible yelled and screamed that his players didn't have the courage to fight back. Before letting his squad return to the field, he pointed at the exit and said, "The first 11 players who go out this door will start the second half! The rest will sit on the bench!" Instantly there was a mad scramble of players for the door. A fight broke out as players tried to push their way out of the locker room. Finally, 11 battle-scarred Nebraska players made it through the exit. Dana Bible's strange pep talk worked. Nebraska went on to beat Indiana, 13–9!

FAMILY TRADITION

The three Wistert Brothers were all college football players who attended the University of Michigan. Francis Wistert started the tradition by playing football at Michigan and winning All-American honors in 1933. Brother Albert went to the University of Michigan and was named an All-American football player in 1942.

The last Wistert brother, Alvin, was a bit late following in his brothers' footsteps. He didn't go to Michigan until 1947, when he was 32 years old. Nevertheless Alvin Wistert also played football, and won All-American honors in 1947 and 1948!

SCORE DETOUR

M any college bowl games have been thrilling, high-scoring contests. But some bowl games have had unusually *low* scores.

The Rose Bowl, which began in 1902, is the granddaddy of all bowl games. It usually has a lot of offensive action. Unfortunately, that was not the case in 1922. In that year's game, the University of California and Washington and Jefferson College played to a dismal 0–0 tie. It is the only game in Rose Bowl history that ended scoreless.

In the 1947 Cotton Bowl, Louisiana State University and Arkansas ended the game deadlocked at 0–0. In 1959, Texas Christian University and the Air Force Academy went to the Cotton Bowl and duplicated that strange feat. They also tied at 0–0.

The Sugar Bowl never had any 0–0 ties, but it came close twice. In 1942 Fordham beat Missouri by the score of 2–0. And in 1936 Texas Christian University edged Louisiana State by the score of 3–2. With those scores in mind, it seems obvious that some teams find it pointless to go "bowling."

GOOD ARM

E d Barrett played a fine game on October 31, 1930, when his Cedartown, Georgia team played the team from Rome, Georgia. Barrett caught four passes and intercepted three. What makes that feat so astonishing is that Barrett had only one arm!

LUCKY LOSS

All Boston College had to do to go to the Sugar Bowl in 1942 was defeat the College of the Holy Cross. Since Boston College was undefeated that season and Holy Cross had won only four games, BC fans figured there was no way Boston College could lose.

Before the game was played, BC supporters scheduled a huge victory celebration at Boston's most famous night club, the Cocoanut Grove. Everything was all set for Boston College's big trip to the Sugar Bowl. Unfortunately, Holy Cross didn't cooperate. They thrashed BC 55–12, and Boston College's Sugar Bowl hopes went right down the drain. The big victory celebration at the Cocoanut Grove was canceled.

However, it was probably the luckiest thing that ever happened to the Boston College players. On the very evening the celebration was supposed to take place, the Cocoanut Grove caught fire. The blaze gutted the building, and 491 people perished. Luckily, no Boston College players were involved in that terrible tragedy—all because the football team had lost to Holy Cross.

UNDERCOVER CALL

In 1895 Auburn University used a trick play to score a touchdown against Vanderbilt. As the Auburn players huddled around their ball carrier, he stuffed the pigskin under his jersey. When the Auburn team scattered, the player with the ball tucked under his shirt scampered for an easy touchdown.

TOO MANY MEN ON THE FIELD

When the game of football first started, there were few rules to govern the sport. Originally, there was not even a set rule about how many players could be on the field for each team. The number of players used by each side was usually agreed upon by both teams before the contest. In the old days there were sometimes as many as 25 players on the field for one team at a time. In 1876, a rule was passed that limited teams to 15 players on the field at a time. It wasn't until 1880 that the modern number of 11 players on each side was established.

ALMOST A HOOP STAR

Joe Montana of the San Francisco 49ers may be one of the greatest quarterbacks ever to play the game of football, but Joe almost became a basketball star instead. When he was a high school player in Monongahela, Pennsylvania, he was going to accept a basketball scholarship to North Carolina State, until Notre Dame offered him a football scholarship.

RUN FOR IT

Coach Gil Dobie of the University of Washington knew how to win football games, but not friends. Once after his Washington team walloped the University of California 72–0, Dobie wasn't satisfied with his squad's performance. He was so mad, in fact, that he made his winning team run 20 laps around the field after the game!

MAKING A SPLASH

When a football player asks for water he's usually thirsty. In 1955 the Baltimore Colts had a way of delivering water that didn't do much to quench a player's thirst. As a joke, Colt veterans would go around dumping buckets of ice-cold water on unsuspecting teammates. The prank was always good for a laugh. Unfortunately head coach Weeb Ewbank got tired of the stunt and outlawed the practice. He even went so far as to threaten to fine the next water thrower $1,000.

Normally a fine like that would discourage most pranksters, but veterans Gino Marchetti and Carl Taseff couldn't resist taking the plunge one more time. They planned to drench rookie fullback Alan Ameche when he walked into the locker room. Taseff hid behind a doorway with a bucket of water while Marchetti stood in plain sight waiting for Ameche to arrive. It was Marchetti's job to signal Taseff when to dump the water. Finally the moment arrived. Marchetti signaled. Quickly Taseff dumped the water on the person who walked through the doorway. However, Gino Marchetti had changed the plan. The person who got dumped on by Carl Taseff was none other than the Colts' head coach, Weeb Ewbank! Luckily for Carl, Weeb had a sense of humor. He accepted Taseff's apology and didn't even fine him!

TICKETS PLEASE

J erry Glanville, who coached the Atlanta Falcons in 1991, had some strange habits when he coached the Houston Oilers in the late 1980's. Glanville would leave free tickets to Houston games at the gate for people who never ever showed up. The reason the people never showed up was because they had passed away years before. Glanville's list for free tickets included Elvis Presley, actor James Dean, and rock singer Buddy Holly. Once, while he was in New York City, Jerry Glanville even had a special pass waiting at the ticket booth for the phantom in *The Phantom of the Opera*. Now that is strange!

HOME-FIELD ADVANTAGE?

M any pro sports teams often talk about having a home-field advantage. Don't tell that to the NFL's Seattle Seahawks. In 1980 the Seahawks lost eight games at the Seattle Kingdome, finishing the season without a single victory on their home turf.

THANKS GUYS

Mel Gray of the St. Louis Cardinals had caught passes in an outstanding 104 consecutive NFL games going into the Cardinals' contest against the Washington Redskins in December 1980. Mel extended his consecutive receiving streak to 105 in that game, but not without a little help from the St. Louis coaches. Gray's only catch came in the fourth quarter and was good for just 3 yards. On that play, Washington was called for a penalty that would have given the Cardinals a pickup of 5 yards. Normally under those circumstances, a team would take the penalty, pick up an additional two yards, and have an extra down to work with. But the Cardinals' coaches decided instead to help Gray keep his streak alive. They refused the penalty and took two less yards on the play so Gray could continue on his merry pass-catching way.

WHAT A BREAK!

In 1924 the University of Washington tied Navy in the Rose Bowl 14–14, thanks to two point-after-touchdown boots by kicker Les Sherman. Kicking those two PAT's was harder than you think. Sherman played the game with a broken toe on his kicking foot. To protect his toe, he wore lots of padding in a shoe four sizes larger than what he normally wore.

MARSHALL MISHAP

All-Pro Jim Marshall made headlines lots of times during his outstanding career. But there was one time in 1964 that Jim made football news for a play he'd rather forget. It happened in a game against the San Francisco 49ers. After a good defensive effort by the Vikings, the 49ers fumbled the ball. Marshall scooped up the pigskin and began to run with it. He headed straight for the end zone. Unfortunately, Marshall had become disoriented during the play and ended up running the wrong way! Despite the yells of his teammates who were trying to stop him, big Jim Marshall rumbled 62 yards with the ball and crossed his own goal line to give the San Francisco 49ers a two-point safety. It was one of the funniest wrong-way runs in NFL history.

BARGAIN TEAM

Can you imagine what it would cost to buy a professional football franchise today? The tab would be in the millions. But back in 1922, when pro teams were first formed into a league, the cost was a lot less. The price tag of a franchise in the American Professional Football Association in 1922 was a mere $100.00!

CONTRACT TALK

In the early days of pro football, the players didn't sign contracts with their teams. The best players often decided to leave one team for another if the pay offered to them was better. Pro players jumped from team to team during the season, which sometimes made things confusing. In 1915, the immortal Knute Rockne was a pro end who frequently switched from team to team. In fact, Rockne played against a pro club called the Columbus Panhandles six times that year—and each time he was on a different team!

LONE SCORER

In a game between the University of Washington and the University of Southern California on December 7, 1935, Washington halfback J. Haines scored all the points on *both* sides of the contest! Haines was tackled behind his goal line for a safety by USC. But later in the contest, he redeemed himself by running for a 25-yard touchdown. That's all the points that were scored that day. Washington won the game 6–2!

MULTI-SPORT STAR

W ay back in 1903, when it was rare to find athletes who played more than one professional sport, a man named Rube Waddell played both pro baseball and pro football. What makes Waddell's feat so interesting is that he played for two pro teams in two different sports in the same city. Rube was a member of the Philadelphia Athletics baseball team, and was later voted into baseball's Hall of Fame. Waddell was also a member of the Philadelphia Athletics pro football team. Another odd twist is that both of the teams were owned by the same man, Connie Mack!

WHERE DID HE GO?

I n 1896 Pat O'Dea tried out for the University of Wisconsin football team and quickly became the squad's star player. O'Dea was a good halfback who won national fame for his ability as a punter and place-kicker. He could kick with the best players of all time, and was soon idolized by fans, coaches, and players alike. By the time he graduated from Wisconsin, Pat was a hero who was recognized everywhere he went.

However, O'Dea didn't like publicity and shied away from attention. He soon dropped out of sight and vanished from the public eye for over 15 years. Everyone thought O'Dea was dead until 17 years later, when he was found living in a small town under the name of Charlie Mitchell. Pat O'Dea had changed his name to escape from his former football fame!

INDOOR GRIDIRON

When people think of football, they usually think of an outdoor sport. However, more and more pro football teams are beginning to play in covered stadiums on artificial turf. The indoor football stadium seems to be the field of the future. Yet the surprising truth is that indoor football is old news. The first indoor football game was played way back in 1902. It was held at Madison Square Garden in New York City. The contest matched a pro team from Syracuse, New York against a pro team from Philadelphia. Three thousand fans showed up to watch Philadelphia win the world's first indoor football game, 6–0.

LONG LIFE

Some people say that football can be hazardous to one's health. Coach Amos Alonzo Stagg lived to be proof that the sport of football may help to promote long life. Stagg, who was born in 1862, coached football for more than 60 years and retired from the sport when he was in his nineties! The famous football coach passed away in 1965 at the age of 102.

TWO-STAR BILLING

Most sports fans know that Knute Rockne was a great college coach at Notre Dame. But he was also a great pro end who played in a pro football championship game for the Massillon (Ohio) Tigers in 1916. The Tigers had earned their way into the title tilt with an explosive offense that featured quarterback Gus Dorais passing to end Knute Rockne. In the championship contest, Massillon took on the Canton (Ohio) Bulldogs. The Bulldogs had a pretty good player of their own. He was former All-American running back Jim Thorpe. How did Rockne fare against Thorpe in the battle of passing versus running? Canton won the championship 29–0, and Jim Thorpe scored all 29 points!

HE'LL GET BETTER

Joe Montana is probably one of the best quarterbacks ever to play the game of football. He starred at the University of Notre Dame and with the San Francisco 49ers. But Joe's potential wasn't recognized in his early playing days. In his freshman year at Notre Dame he was the seventh-string signal caller!

GREAT GOING, GRANDSON!

Many people know that Brigham Young University is named after Mormon leader Brigham Young. BYU is also famous for its great football teams. In 1979 Steve Young became a part of the school's history in more ways than one. He was a quarterback at the school named after his great-great-grandfather.

LUCKY BREAK

The famous Carlisle College for Indians took on the U.S. Military Academy in a football game on November 9, 1912. Led by legendary running back Jim Thorpe, Carlisle walloped the Cadets of Army 27–6.

During the game, something strange happened. It turned out to be a head-on meeting between two famous men. When Carlisle had the ball, Thorpe took a hand-off and ran for the goal line. A young Army cadet tried to stop him with a bruising tackle. The cadet crashed into Thorpe, but instead of stopping him, ended up breaking his own leg. The name of the cadet was Dwight David Eisenhower, who went on to become a great general and eventually president of the United States. The broken leg ended Eisenhower's football career, but he went on to fame nevertheless.

SMILE WHEN YOU SAY THAT

J ohn Brailler was a tough football player for West Virginia University and later for an early pro team in Latrobe, Pennsylvania. In fact Brailler was one of the first players to be paid to play football. Brailler, who later quit football and became a dentist, was such a tough player that some people said he only quit knocking opponents' teeth out on the gridiron so he could yank them out in his office!

BIG MISTAKE

J ohn Elway of the Denver Broncos is a superstar quarterback. He is a great leader who has taken his team to the Super Bowl. But even great players have bad days. In Elway's rookie season in 1983, his Denver Broncos were demolished by the San Diego Chargers, 31–7. John Elway was sacked several times and chased around the field all day by the Chargers' defense. Things were so bad during the game that a confused John Elway made a funny mistake. When his team had the ball, Elway lined up behind his offensive guard to take the snap, instead of behind his center. After his teammates yelled to him, an embarrassed John Elway shifted behind the correct lineman.

GLIDING ALONG

In 1979 the University of California Golden Bears had an outstanding quarterback named Rich Campbell, whom opponents just couldn't seem to stop. However, in a game against USC that season, Campbell was almost knocked out of the game. It happened as Rich was running over to the sidelines to speak to his coach. Campbell heard the crowd roar and looked up just in time. A man on a hang glider had crashed the game without permission and was sailing right at the young quarterback. Campbell quickly dropped to all fours as the glider narrowly missed crashing into him!

WELL COVERED

Super Bowl I was played on January 15, 1967, and the game between the National Football League and American Football League champions was well covered by TV. Since the NFL and AFL had contracts with different TV networks, the contest was broadcast by both CBS and NBC!

JUST LIKE HOME

In 1975 John McKay, Jr. was a receiver on the USC football team. Playing for the University of Southern California Trojans made John feel right at home. USC's quarterback was Pat Haden, John's old high-school quarterback and friend. And the coach of the Trojans that year was John McKay, Sr., John Jr.'s father.

UH OH!

Don Shula is one of the most respected men to ever coach a pro football team. But his career in the NFL didn't exactly get off to a good start. In 1960 Shula's first pro coaching job was with the Detroit Lions. He was the Lions' defensive coach. Shula got a chance to make his first call as an NFL coach in a game against the Cleveland Browns on August 14, 1960. When the Browns offense got the ball for the first time, Shula signaled in what defense he wanted. That call proved to be a baptism under fire for Don Shula. The pass coverage he called wasn't quite right, and the Browns scored a touchdown on the very first play.

DRIVING ME CRAZY

In 1923 Penn State University almost missed the biggest game of the season. The team was late arriving at the Rose Bowl game, because the team bus got stuck in traffic on the way to the stadium. If that wasn't bad enough, Penn State's head coach, Hugo Bezdek, and USC's head coach, Gus Henderson, got into an argument over the incident when the Penn State squad finally did arrive. The argument was so intense that the two coaches almost got into a fistfight before the kickoff.

HEADS UP

Joe Guyon and Jim Thorpe were playing for the Canton (Ohio) Bulldogs when they cooked up a scheme to send opposing halfback Fritz Pollard of the Akron (Ohio) Pros out of the game. Guyon and Thorpe planned to converge on Pollard from opposite sides when Fritz fielded a punt and knock him silly. During the game Joe and Jim got their chance to nail Fritz when Canton punted. Thorpe and Guyon charged at Pollard as he caught the ball. However, the plan didn't work. Fritz Pollard ducked and Joe Guyon and Jim Thorpe smashed into each other, knocking themselves out of the game!

WHEEL BAD BREAK

E veryone knows that pro football can be a dangerous sport. And that pro linebackers just might be the toughest players in the game. What coach Marty Schottenheimer of the Kansas City Chiefs didn't know was that scooters can be dangerous, too. In 1991 Schottenheimer allowed his players to ride small scooters around the Wisconsin-River Falls college campus, where the Chiefs held their preseason camp that year. Unfortunately, the Chiefs' top draft pick, linebacker Percy Snow, was riding a scooter when he cracked up and fractured his ankle. He had to undergo surgery for bone and ligament damage. After the incident Schottenheimer decided players would no longer be able to ride the scooters. They were just too dangerous!

FLUSHED

D efensive end John Matuszak, who played for the Kansas City Chiefs and the Oakland Raiders, was not only big, but strong, too. He once demonstrated his strength by yanking a toilet out of a hotel bathroom.

MAGIC 33

The number 33 isn't exactly a magic number to football players at Bernardsville High School in New Jersey. On October 5, 1991, Bernardsville lost to Glen Ridge High School. The loss was the 33rd straight defeat suffered by hapless Bernardsville. What made matters worse was the final score of that contest. Glen Ridge won the game, 33–0.

GRAVE PROBLEM

Al "Bubba" Baker of the Detroit Lions learned the fundamentals of football on a strange playing field. As a youngster, Baker and his friends couldn't find an open field to play on, so their football games were played in a cemetery between the tombstones.

EVERYBODY'S PICK

D ave Logan was a popular player with pro scouts. In 1976 the University of Colorado star receiver was a high draft pick of the NFL's Cleveland Browns. But Logan was also drafted as a basketball player by the NBA's Kansas City Kings and as a baseball player by the National League's Cincinnati Reds! Logan was flattered by all the attention, but chose to play football for the Browns.

POST PATTERN

T he 1927 Rose Bowl ended in a 7–7 tie between the University of Alabama and Stanford University.

BONK!

Alabama had an excellent chance to win the game, but what prevented an Alabama victory was a strange twist of fate. In the second quarter, Stanford halfback Dick Hyland retreated into his own end zone after fielding a punt at the five-yard line, and was about to be tackled for a two-point safety, when a weird event saved him. The player who was about to tackle Hyland accidentally ran into the goalpost and knocked himself out, and Hyland was able to make it back to the 20-yard line!

FOOT-IN-MOUTH PLAY

O n October 29, 1965, Jay Estabrook was the punter for Tufts University in a game against Amherst College. Estabrook was called in to punt with a 25-mile-per-hour wind blowing into his face. To his surprise, his kick sailed high up into the air and then blew right back at him. Estabrook caught his own punt, and was then tackled by an Amherst defender for a four-yard loss!

DREAM ON

O ffensive guard Tom Glassic of the Denver Broncos was almost too well rested for the 1978 Super Bowl. Glassic's Bronco squad took on the Dallas Cowboys at the New Orleans Superdome for the world championship that season. Before the game, Tom visited his parents' New Orleans hotel room and decided to lie down to take a nap. Unfortunately, his snooze lasted longer than expected, and when he woke up, his Denver teammates had already left for the stadium on the team bus! Tom would have been late for the Super Bowl if a police officer hadn't given him a lift to the Superdome in a squad car.

ONE-CATCH CAREER

If you could play wide receiver in the NFL and make only one catch during your entire career, wouldn't you want that catch to come in the Super Bowl? That's just what happened to Percy Howard of the Dallas Cowboys in 1976. Howard was a rookie receiver for the Cowboys that year and hadn't caught a single pass all season. In Super Bowl X against the Pittsburgh Steelers, Percy snared a 34-yard touchdown pass from Roger Staubach. Unfortunately, he didn't catch another pass in the game, and the following year Howard suffered an injury that forced him to retire from pro football. His one and only catch as a pro was a TD reception in the Super Bowl!

WHAT'S THE POINT?

The University of Michigan and Stanford University met in the 1972 Rose Bowl. Going into the contest, mighty Michigan felt Stanford wouldn't stand a chance. After all, even though Stanford was in the Rose Bowl, they'd lost to San Jose State by a score of 13–12 during the regular season, and everyone knew that San Jose State wasn't a football powerhouse. As you might expect, Michigan's overconfidence was a grave mistake. Stanford went on to beat Michigan in the 1972 Rose Bowl on a last-second field goal. Strangely enough, the final score was 13–12, exactly the same score that Stanford had lost to San Jose State by earlier that year.

PIGSKIN PEEL-OFF

When Dick Vermeil took over as head coach of the Philadelphia Eagles, he had an ocean of enthusiasm but only a trickle of patience for players who didn't see things his way. Vermeil ran tough practices and didn't like to hear complaints. During the 1980 season, Vermeil became so exasperated with a free-agent guard that he completely lost his temper. He ordered the director of player personnel to cut the youngster right there in the middle of practice—which the director did.

After hearing the bad news, the guard made one of the funniest exits in NFL history. As he slowly walked off the field, he peeled off his equipment bit by bit and dropped it in his wake. By the time he reached the locker room he was wearing nothing but shorts, and had left behind a trail of gridiron gear for the equipment manager to collect.

REVERSE RUN

The most famous wrong-way run in college football history took place during the 1929 Rose Bowl between Georgia Tech and the University of California Golden Bears. After a Georgia Tech fumble, California lineman Roy Riegels picked up the pigskin and dashed off in the wrong direction toward his own end zone. Riegels was stopped one yard short of scoring a safety for Georgia Tech. He was tackled by one of his teammates on the one-yard line.

YOUNG PLAYERS

In 1926 the Milwaukee franchise of the brand-new National Football League was fined $500 for using four illegal players on their pro team. The four players were local high school boys!

WHAT'S IN A NAME?

Because of money problems, the Philadelphia Eagles and the Pittsburgh Steelers merged to form a single team in 1943. That team was called the Phil-Pitt Eagles. They eventually went back to being the two teams we know today.

YOU AGAIN?

Running back James Bettis stood 5' 9" and weighed only 160 pounds when he tried out for the University of Cincinnati football team in 1978. The coaches thought Bettis was too small and cut him from the squad after just one practice.

However, James Bettis refused to take no for an answer. He returned to try out again the next year. Not only did he make the team that year, but he ended up being the team's leading rusher that season. By the time Bettis finished playing for Cincinnati, he'd etched his name into the school's record books. The guy who'd originally been cut after a single practice became the school's all-time leading rusher!

TIMELY PLAY

In 1975 quarterback Joe Montana of Notre Dame entered a game against North Carolina with his team down by the score of 14–6. Since it was late in the fourth quarter, things looked bleak for Notre Dame. However, Montana didn't see it that way. He led his team to a quick touchdown on five plays, and then threw for a two-point conversion to tie the score at 14–14. His next time on the field, he tossed an 80-yard touchdown pass. Notre Dame won by a score of 21–14. Amazingly, Montana helped his team score two TD's and a two-point conversion to win the game in a time span of only one minute and two seconds!

PRINCETON JINX

The first college football game took place on November 6, 1869. It was played between Princeton and Rutgers. Rutgers won that first game, 6–4, but Princeton managed to even the score after that first defeat. In fact, for the next 68 games in a row—from 1870 to 1938—Princeton won every single football contest between the two schools!

LETTER IMPERFECT

North Carolina State was a big underdog for its football contest against Wake Forest in 1939. To try to generate some enthusiasm and motivation for winning, NC State assistant coach Herman Hickman cooked up a crazy scheme. He wrote mean, nasty, threatening letters to all the starting members of the North Carolina State team and signed each letter, "A Wake Forest Player." Hickman hoped the letters would make the State players mad enough to pull off a stunning upset. Unfortunately, the letter-writing plan didn't work. Wake Forest walloped NC State, 32–0!

UP IN ARMS

The 1893 Army-Navy football game was more of a slugfest than a sporting event. The gridiron clash was marred by fights and brawls. When Navy won the game 6–4, an Army general on the sidelines punched a nearby Navy admiral who had insulted the Army cadets. The angry admiral then challenged the general to a shooting duel, which later took place in secret. Luckily, no one was hurt. However, when President Grover Cleveland learned about the dueling incident, he ordered the Army-Navy football game discontinued for the next six years!

FACE IT

Grabbing another player's face mask can be very dangerous. However, up until 1962 grabbing the face mask of any NFL player except a ball carrier was perfectly legal. The rule wasn't changed to include all players until January 9, 1962!

WRIST BANDITS

Quarterback Jimmy Field of Louisiana State University wore a wristband with all of his team's offensive plays written on it for their game against Florida State University in 1960. The wristband was supposed to help Field call a better game against Florida State. However, it didn't work out that way.

During a pileup in the first half, Field was tackled and his wristband was accidentally ripped off. The wristband was lost in the shuffle, and none of the LSU players or coaches gave it a second thought.

In the second half of the game, Florida State's defense completely dominated the LSU offense. In fact, Florida State rallied from a 10–7 score to win the game 13–10. It wasn't until the game was over that LSU found out that the Florida State defenders had found Jimmy Field's wristband and had used it to shut down the LSU offense!

TIME

The 1963 Rose Bowl in Pasadena, California matched the Wisconsin Badgers against the USC Trojans. The game was in full swing when play was suddenly halted as the teams lined up to begin a new play. Someone had called a time-out. But it wasn't called by the offense, the defense, *or* the officials! The time-out was called by an excited TV technician who ran out onto the field. The game was being carried live by television and it was time for a commercial!

PIGSKIN PUNISHMENT

After Notre Dame player Johnny Lattner fumbled five times in a game against Purdue in 1952, Coach Frank Leahy came up with an unusual punishment for his star halfback. He had a special football made with a handle attached to it, and made Lattner carry it around the Notre Dame campus.

NUMBER-ONE JINX

Most teams would love to be ranked #1 in the college football polls. But there was one year when it seemed that being named #1 was a sure way to lose! At least that's what happened five times in a row in the 1981 season. Michigan started the season ranked #1 in the nation and was promptly upset by Wisconsin. Notre Dame moved into the #1 spot the next week and was then dumped by Michigan. The University of Southern California became the next #1 pick and ended up losing to Arizona State. Then Texas was named the #1 team in the country. They immediately lost to Arkansas. Finally, Penn State jumped into the #1 slot. Naturally they ended up being upset by Miami. Who says being #1 is the greatest?

FOOTBALL BROADCAST

Quarterback Steve DeBerg of the San Francisco 49ers had a voice problem in 1980. A bruised larynx kept the sound of his voice to just above a whisper. DeBerg found that he couldn't call signals loudly enough for his teammates to hear in a noisy stadium. But that didn't prevent Steve from running the offense in a game against the New Orleans Saints. The 49ers got permission from the NFL to wire DeBerg's equipment with a special microphone and amplifier that would allow him to broadcast signals to his teammates. The microphone helped DeBerg lead San Francisco to a 24–21 win over New Orleans.

WEDDING MARCH

Duke Hanny of the Chicago Bears wanted to get married during the 1925 football season. Hanny asked Coach George Halas for permission to miss a game so he could be wed. Halas, who lived and breathed football, refused to let Duke skip the game. But that didn't stop the wedding. Hanny showed up for the game but got into a fight after the opening kickoff. He was promptly booted out of the contest by the officials. Since he could no longer play in the game, Duke left the stadium and made it to his wedding on time. Some people say Duke Hanny staged his little fight on purpose. What do you think?

TIME TO GO HOME

In Indiana, high school football games never end in a tie. Teams play overtime periods until a winner is determined. In 1979 St. Rita's of Cincinnati and the Indiana School for the Deaf were deadlocked in a gridiron battle that just didn't want to end. The two teams played *seven* overtime periods before the Indiana School for the Deaf finally ended up the 24–18 victor in the contest.

SPEED TRAP

Defensive tackle Art Donovan was a great player, but not very fast. When Donovan starred for the Baltimore Colts, Coach Weeb Ewbank used him as an early test for rookie linemen. Donovan was matched up against the rookies in a foot race. Any rookies who were outrun by Donovan were considered by Coach Ewbank to be too slow to make it to the pros and were released.

POE BOYS

Writer Edgar Allan Poe was a master of the horror story. But there was nothing horrible about the Poe family when it came to playing football. Six descendants of the famous American writer starred on the gridiron as varsity players for Princeton University.

BED MATE

Tackle Ron McLeon of the Cal State-Fullerton football team always slept with football on his mind. In fact, he never went to bed before a game without taking his football equipment with him. Ron would place his pads on the mattress next to him. His cleats were laid at the foot of the bed. On a pillow next to his own he placed his helmet. Some people say politics makes odd bedfellows. What about football?

PIGSKIN POLICE

Jack Lambert was a star linebacker for the Pittsburgh Steelers in 1980. That same year Lambert was given a star by the Pittsburgh Police Department and made an honorary Pittsburgh police officer. Jack was issued badge #58 by the police to match the number 58 he wore on his football jersey. Lambert was so honored for giving the Pittsburgh Police Department lots of good publicity. He had worn a police baseball cap during his appearance at the Super Bowl that year.

BRANCHING OUT

In 1920 Ursinus College decided to build a football stadium. But there was a slight problem. A huge sycamore tree, almost 200 years old, was right where the field would be. Rather than chop down the grand old tree, planners decided to keep the tree and lay out the field so the leafy giant could remain standing. Thus the tree ended up staying at the end of the football field inside the stadium for almost 65 years. In 1984 a freak storm knocked over the 250-year-old hardwood, much to the sorrow of players and fans alike.

ALL WET

F ielding Yost was one of the greatest football coaches in the history of the game. At the University of Michigan, Yost coached for many years and had several top teams, including a sensational undefeated squad in 1901.

Coach Yost was a great motivator who was well known for his fiery pep talks during halftime. Once, however, Yost's ability to fire up his team put the damper on the squad's performance in the second half. During halftime of an important Big Ten contest, Fielding Yost worked his team into a fever pitch. At the end of his talk, Yost yelled, "Men of Michigan! Now is the time to go out that door to victory!" Yost stood up and made the mistake of pointing to the wrong door.

The Michigan team jumped up and raced through the door, which led to a swimming pool. Before the stampede of young men could be halted, several players actually fell into the pool and had to be fished out.

The surprise dunking of the Michigan squad cooled their enthusiasm and fire. They ended up losing the game.

BUSY DAY

T he University of Texas beat the University of Missouri 40–27 in the 1946 Cotton Bowl. It was a busy afternoon for Texas quarterback Bobby Layne. He personally had a hand in *every point* his team scored in victory. Layne scored four rushing touchdowns, kicked four extra points, and threw two touchdown passes!

SHOUT IT OUT!

When Princeton met Rutgers in the first-ever college football game in 1869, Princeton came up with a novel plan. Princeton players were told to yell and scream during the game to distract the Rutgers players. Unfortunately, the yelling didn't work, and Rutgers went on to win 6–4. The next year the teams met again and this time Princeton modified its plan. They brought along spectators who were part of a special cheering section. On hand to do the yelling and hollering, those spectators were probably the world's first football cheerleaders. By the way, the plan worked in 1870. Princeton won the game, 8–0.

BENCHED

T alk about strange rules. Up until 1944 it was illegal for an NFL coach to shout plays to his offensive team. It was in 1944 that coaching from the bench was finally made legal in the NFL.

SEA SICK

I n 1980 head football coach Don Ruggeri of the Massachusetts Maritime Academy in Buzzards Bay, Massachusetts had a problem. He had to open his football season with 42 veteran members of his squad out at sea in conjunction with their schooling as merchant marines. Ruggeri had to play the first 5 games with 6 senior and 32 freshman ball players. He was certainly glad when his players' ship finally came in. But having his team out to sea really didn't matter that much. The Academy's rookie players had earned an outstanding 4–1 record by the time the veterans finally got their feet on solid ground again.

GREATEST COMEBACK

O ne of the most remarkable comebacks in NFL history occurred in a game between the San Francisco 49ers and the New Orleans Saints on December 7, 1980. Trailing the Saints 35–7 at half-time, the 49ers roared back to score 31 unanswered points in the second half—and won the game 38–35! The 49ers had overcome the largest deficit (28 points) in NFL history.

THE NEW YORK WHO?

Every good sports fan knows that the New York Yankees are a baseball team, but did you know there was once a pro football team also called the New York Yankees? In 1946 the New York Yankees pro-football team played in the All-American Conference, a rival league of the NFL. Unfortunately, the Yanks couldn't compete with the drawing power of the NFL's New York Giants and soon folded as a team.

BOOTED OUT

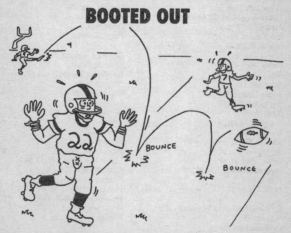

In 1937 kicker Bruno Konopka of Manual High School in Denver, Colorado set an amazing high-school kicking record. Bruno punted a football some 77 yards in the air. The ball hit the ground and kept bouncing. When it finally stopped rolling, a measurement was taken. Bruno Konopka's punt had traveled an amazing 132 yards, 6 inches!

However, Bruno didn't have much to celebrate when the game was over. He later missed a point-after-touchdown kick in the contest, and his team lost the game, 7–6!

INDEX